Barbara Woodhouse

on

HANDLING A PROBLEM DOG

RINGPRESS

RINGPRESS

Published by Ringpress Books Ltd,
Spirella House, Bridge Road,
Letchworth, Herts, SG6 4ET

Discounts available for bulk orders
Contact the Special Sales Manager at
the above address. Telephone (0462) 674177

First Published 1992

ISBN 0 948955 67 8

Printed and bound in Singapore
by Kyodo Printing Co

CONTENTS

FOREWORD

By Patrick Woodhouse

My mother was born in Ireland in 1910 at a boys' public school where her father was headmaster. Both her family and the boys at the school had a great many different animals and thus she grew up surrounded by them from a very early age. Dogs and other animals became so much a part of her life that it was obvious from the start that she would have animals around her all her life.

One of my earliest recollections of my mother was that she was always with one or other of her two dogs. In the early Fifties she had a Great Dane which responded so perfectly to her training that it won numerous prizes for obedience work. She realised that she really did have a gift for training dogs and she decided that she must use this gift to help others train their dogs. She started professionally in 1951 with a dog training club meeting on Croxley Green, just a few yards from our house, which was called Campions. She soon had a class of 25-30 dogs and their owners every Sunday and this led to the founding of four other training clubs, in nearby towns, which were always full of dog owners wishing to learn. Her weekends and evenings were thus spent doing the thing she enjoyed most, the training of dogs.

Her own Great Danes, Juno and Junia, were trained to such a highstandard that they could work in films and on TV programmes by just being shown the action. Then by simply giving them a command or signal, they would act out the part to perfection. Juno, mother's best known Great Dane, became known as " Take 1 Juno" on the sets of the studios where she worked with famous actors like Sir Alec Guinness, Clark Gable, Roger Moore, Eric Morecambe, and many others. Her Great Danes acted in more than eighty TV and movie productions in their careers, and many of the films were produced by my mother and often directed by her as well.

Her career really started to take off when she was invited to do a TV series about dog training for the BBC and the series was to be called: Training Dogs The Woodhouse Way. This series became such a success that it was repeated three times during its first year and led to two more series and a host of appearances on other programmes in which she was interviewed and in which she demonstrated her methods of dog training to TV stars such as Terry Wogan and Michael Parkinson. In the United States the programmes of her dog training became so popular that they are still being shown to this very day. She became known as the "Dog Lady" and her books became some of the best-sellers ever known in America. In 1980 she won the cherished TV award presented by the Pye Corporation as the Female TV Personality Of The Year and went on to win the title of the World's Best Dog Trainer. Since those hectic days she has travelled the world demonstrating her methods to countless dog owners and visiting numerous countries, including the United States of America, Canada, Australia, New Zealand, Singapore and many parts of Europe, before her death in 1988 following a stroke.

I hope that you, the reader, will get a great deal of help from this book and that it will answer all your questions about the difficulties many people experience when training their dogs. I am sure that the sense of achievement you will experience when you have successfully trained your dog to do even the simplest of exercises will give you a sense of oneness with your dog that cannot be bettered by a relationship with any other animal. May I wish you every success with your training and hope that your dog will become, to quote my mother: "A DOG THAT IS A PLEASURE TO ALL AND A NUISANCE TO NO ONE."

There is no need for a 'bad dog' if the owner is prepared to give it the discipline and training it requires, says Barbara Woodhouse.

Chapter One

WHY BAD DOGS?

When I had finished the manuscript of my book on training dogs I sent it to my mother. Her remark after reading it was that although she had enjoyed it as a book, she felt certain no one would need it, as surely everyone knew how to train their dogs. Time has shown that not only do people not know how to train their dogs, but that in increasing numbers they own 'problem dogs' and are in need of specialised help and advice. In the hundreds of letters I receive the phrase 'difficult dog' occurs time and time again. Many of the writers tell me that they have owned dogs for thirty years or more and have never come up against such stubborn, 'wilful, vicious', or such-like dogs before. They all, without exception, imagine that their dog stands out on its own as a unique example of canine wickedness. If only they could read my daily post they would know their letters are repeated almost word for word by many hundreds of dog owners all over the world. What they are unwilling to believe at first is that their dog is no worse than dozens of others, and that if it is 'difficult', the reason can often be placed on their own doorstep. I still maintain, and always shall maintain, that with the exception of dogs which have some physical or mental abnormality, there is not one that cannot be made a good companion by the right training – that is *if* the owner can be trained. During the last ten years I have trained 15,000 dogs and owners, and my heart bleeds for the so-called problem dogs brought to me for correction. In most cases the dog can be taught all that is necessary in a very few minutes. When I start to work, using a thrilling happy tone of voice, the dog works happily with tail wagging and an expectant interested look on his face. When he errs I use the tone of voice that means 'I win or else' and few dogs fail to recognise that voice and that look on my face. But hand this same dog back to his inexperienced owner and the picture changes. Why?

Firstly because it is the nature of our people in recent years to put up with more from our children and our dogs. Next, kindness to animals has been drummed into us as a nation for a long time, and many owners mix up in their minds the true meaning of kindness. Is it kinder to allow a dog to make human lives and his own a misery, rather than to correct him firmly on a choke chain for a few minutes, thereby making him understand clearly who is boss? I wouldn't hesitate to answer this question. I would say, 'Correct the dog quickly and firmly, and then love him with everything you possess, and the dog will worship you in return.' Dither weakly in the mistaken idea that all bad dogs can be trained by endearing words and you might just as well give up the idea of training a 'bad dog'. Remember, writing this I am not dealing with the normal puppy or young dog, or with the experienced owner to whom training a dog is as easy as eating his breakfast.

There is no doubt in my mind that, due to the vast increase in the number of dogs kept in this country, and the conditions under which these dogs are housed, a type of dog that should never have been bred is being produced by breeders for sale to the public. The professional breeders cannot be excused for doing this. They should know better than to breed from bitches or dogs with bad temperaments, thus passing on trouble. The amateur breeders still believe the old wives' tale that to breed from a nervous or bad-tempered bitch improves her temperament. What they don't know or don't care about is that they are filling this country with unstable, neurotic and unreliable dogs which are causing thousands of dog lovers misery, and keeping me and others like me glued to our typewriters and our training classes, trying to right the wrongs that should never be met with in normal dogs. But in spite of what I say about the breeding of these

dogs, I still believe that if the owners knew how to train them these faults could easily and quickly be eradicated.

There is however one thing I cannot teach a dog, and that is to love his owner. I meet many hundreds of dogs in a year who seem to have no affection for their owner whatsoever. These dogs have to be taught to obey their owners more or less by fear of the results of disobedience. How very sad it is to find such a relationship. It tears my heart-strings when the dog's eyes light up when he meets me, and he shrieks with joy when I kneel down to caress and kiss him. How is it possible to feed and house a dog, and presumably to love it, and get no affection in return? The answer is respect. Without respect there is little love in the animal kingdom. An animal must always have a boss to love and respect. Some breeds of dog need to respect their owners more than others, some are naturally docile and obedient.

I am going to deal with the many types of problem that are presented to me by dog owners in person or by letter. On reading what I say many indignant owners will deny that they come under any of the categories I mention. Many more will insist that their dog is more wicked than any of those that I talk about, and that theirs could not be cured by the means I recommend. Some will write to me and say they have tried everything and are quite sure that their dog would be my Waterloo. I willingly accept such challenges, if the owners are willing to bring their dog to me for five minutes. For in those five minutes I will find out who is to blame for the 'problem dog', and if I think there is no future happiness for dog and owner in that particular partnership, I will admit it quite freely. For make no mistake, there is no future in many of these dog and owner relationships. The reasons are numerous; one of the most common is a fear of the dog, fear of the dog fighting, or biting, or both. Unless the owner can master his own fear there is no hope for the dog. The variations on the problems are numerous, but in spite of what people think, the same training works for all the different vices. Naturally every dog and owner has slightly different troubles which may need slight variations in handling, but the principle does not vary.

Chapter Two

PROBLEM OWNERS

My casebook is full of owners of every description. Over-sentimental owners, owners in need themselves of immediate psychiatric help, owners who never should be owners, and owners who have problems but who respond immediately to help given, and their lives have thereby been changed for the better. There are owners who wish to imprint their ideas on me rather than letting me imprint my ideas on them, owners who come to me when they are tired of their dogs and wish me to endorse that I think their dogs should be put to sleep, and get downright angry when I say the dog is easily cured of any fault and I attempt to do the remedy at once.

One lady drove up in a car and said her dog was impossible, fought every dog he met and would do nothing right, and her husband would only have him put to sleep if I said the dog was untrainable. This was a Bull Terrier, a breed known for its aggressive attitude towards other dogs, but in this case there was absolutely nothing wrong with the dog at all. I mixed him with dogs, freed him with dogs, did the 'long down' with other dogs, and found him a highly intelligent, highly obedient and loving animal. I refused to endorse her wish for me to write to her husband and say he was untrainable. This story had a happy ending, the lady came on a course and learnt to love the dog instead of finding him a bore, but not many cases have happy endings.

The worst cases come under the the the title of phobias, and those who project their own faults in character make-up to their dogs. One lady arrived with a tiny Poodle who she said had a terrible fear of loud noises, hated water, and would not go on a bus or a car without terror in her heart. The moment the owner stepped out of the car with a subdued husband following in the background, I knew where the fault lay. I put a choke chain on the dog and walked her down the road to a building site, where huge lorries were tipping their loads with tremendous noise, every few minutes. The dog's tail was up; she was sniffing all the exciting country scents in a typical untroubled doggy manner, and the falling bricks and huffs and puffs of compressors etc had not the slightest effect on her. The next thing I did was to put dog and owners into my car and drive to a huge lake near us, which was supposed to be so "eerie" that the dog would be terrified. I let the dog off the lead and raced around with her, throwing sticks for her to retrieve, and then said "Patty, go into the water and have a drink," which she promptly did, and paddled quite happily until I called her out. I told the owner that as far as Patty was concerned, there were no phobias in her life; all were in the lady's imagination, and she was trying to project her own phobias about noise and eerie water into the dog's mind. On returning to my home, the lady remarked to my husband, who is a doctor, that I had said *she* was a nutcase. I hope I had shown her who it was to blame. I pointed out that with the proper choke chain, a few good jerks should the dog do anything wrong, and possibly a paddle in the lake with the dog by her, there would be no problem with the dog. All the dog needed was healthy open air walks, a happy outlook on the owner's part, and no ideas of any abnormality of temperament from the owner. Two days later my choke chain came back through the post, so I suppose anything I had done was completely disregarded. I had an idea the root of the trouble in this case was a wife one, not a dog owner one.

One of the most pathetic cases I coped with was the desire of a woman to have a child substitute in the form of a dog. Dogs are not child substitutes; they are dogs with all the individuality that dogs possess. One can love them as one does a child, one can train them up to almost human standards and teach them to reason out things which many people say is impossible, but I have proved it with my own dogs, many a time. Dogs reason, if the brain is highly developed from the moment they come into the house. I am appalled at the number of dogs whose eyes show little intelligence, whose knowledge of the meaning of words and thoughts is strangely lacking, and whose main idea is either copulation or hunting, the owner only being a useful appendage for the essentials in life and the guarding of the owner's home. It is sad how much these owners have missed in companionship and achievement in understanding their dog. But of course, to train a dog to a high standard of intelligence as well as obedience takes as much time and understanding as teaching a five-year-old child the three Rs. Many owners are far too flat in their characters ever to achieve this standard of intelligence in their dogs. They may be too sentimental, they may abandon training too quickly, with the idea that their dog doesn't like training. Dogs like training if the owners are exciting enough, the best owners are outgoing, full of fun, yet gentle and loving as well as firm, and if necessary appearing angry if the dog transgresses.

Recently a man drove a long way to see me with a Golden Retriever, which he said refused to come out of the car, and pulled terribly to get back into it if ejected forcibly. The dog was terrifically fat, which made the handling of him an almost impossible feat, really needing a strong, young man to achieve the jerks that the dog should have had on the choke chain to put sense into him. They had a short lead, the wrong thin-linked choke chain, which would have hurt the

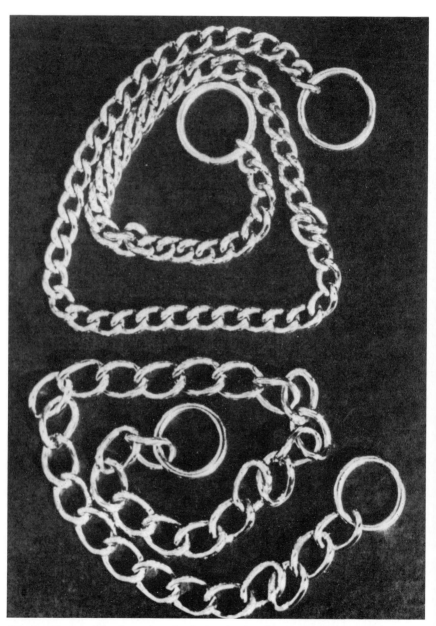

Choke chains: The broader the link, the kinder to the dog.

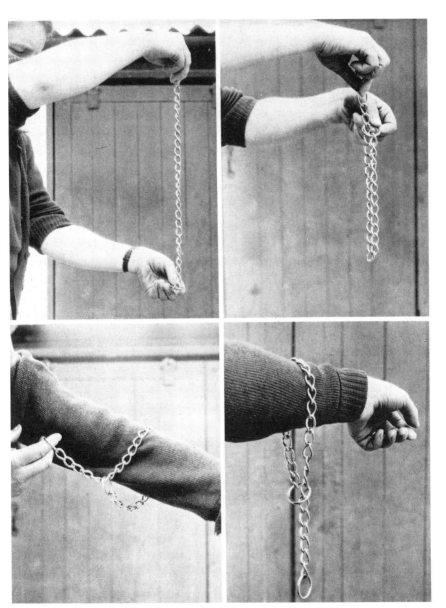

To use: (1) Hold by both rings. (2) Drop chain through one ring. (3) Put on dog pulling upwards. (4) The chain automatically loosens when used correctly.

Correct: The proper way to use a choke chain.

Wrong: A chain incorrectly put on a dog.

dog had it been closed on the neck, and the attitude on arriving here was 'I know you can't cure this.' The first thing I did was to put my own thick-linked choke chain on the dog, and a four foot strong lead. I opened the door of the estate car, and called the dog by name with a commanding voice and a very welcoming voice alternating. The dog just stayed lying down trembling in the car, so I got tough. I said: "Randy, come" and with a very sharp downward jerk on his choke chain, the dog bounced out in one leap. Then I praised him and let him get back into the car again. The shivering started again, so I repeated this action three times, and then took the dog for a walk. As he

pulled so terribly on the lead, walks for this dog had, I was told, been impossible. The only freedom he ever got was when they could get him out of the car in some safe place and let him run about, when he would immediately head back for the car and stay shivering outside.

The jerks on the choke chain did the trick. The dog's tail rose from between his legs, he stopped pulling on the lead, and when we eventually returned to the car, I opened the back and the dog jumped in and lay down. I gave the command "Randy, come" and the dog leapt out, anticipating another fun walk, which he got. After that there was never any trouble about shivering or not wanting to get out of the car. I suggested the dog was put on a diet immediately to make the effort of going for a nice long walk less tiring for Randy, and less risk to his heart, as he was a three-year-old dog.

The phobias I meet are very often connected with the show ring. Dogs that won't be handled by judges, by men or women, and who would all be champions according to their owners, if only they would stand for examination, not bite the judge, stay put on a table, keep their tail up while being looked at, or wouldn't sit in the ring. This may sound a tall order to accomplish, yet in fact, it all starts with the same routine obedience. The dogs that won't be handled by a judge must have a thick-linked choke chain, even if it is a 1 1/2 lb Chihuahua. Sentimental talk about the chain being too heavy carries no weight with me; the chains only weigh 2 1/2 oz, so that even a Chihuahua can carry that load without too much discomfort. I consider the thin show leads are far more uncomfortable for the dogs. In my opinion, the idea that the correct choke chain is cruel and that dogs don't like them is nonsense. I can understand the wrong kind being cruel, like the spiked collars or the very thin-linked ones. Very large linked choke chains are quite harmless; in my opinion most choke chains are used wrongly. The correct method of using a choke chain in my school is a sharp downward jerk, this blocking the release, which in my type of chain makes a loud click. This I term 'pup music' for it has a very happy effect on dogs.

If the owner is too protective, a puppy will gain no-self-confidence.

Chapter Three

NERVOUS DOGS

When a puppy first comes to his new owner he is probably a tiny mite and the mistress of his destiny pours out all her mother love, and sympathises with his fears; he is taken everywhere with her, or someone stays at home to make him feel he is not deserted. Most probably he is allowed the luxury of sleeping under the eiderdown of his new owner's bed, because he is so tiny and helpless, and his cries are so pathetic. If he is a small dog his fear of traffic is overcome by being carried in the town, his unwillingness to walk amongst big feet is sympathised with by the owner who uses endearing words of encouragement to help him take his first steps in this big terrifying world of traffic and feet. The result is the puppy gains no self-confidence, it is all boosted confidence given to him by the owner using comforting words and carrying him. Should one ever try to give the dog confidence by firm jerks and a confident happy voice, paying no attention to him, sitting down and refusing to walk, then one is bound to meet the over-sentimental, and ill-educated, so-called dog lover, who will in a loud voice

accuse you of being cruel to a tiny puppy. Few owners can retaliate in public, so the best thing to do is to ignore such people and carry on with what you are doing, in the knowledge that only by ignoring the puppy's fears will you help him to overcome them. Walk firmly on, speaking happily to the puppy or nervous dog, making him come on with quick jerks, and very soon you will have helped him over his first hurdle – fear.

I cure many dogs that will not show themselves at dog shows owing to nerves; dogs that will not be handled by men and dogs that are terrified of bangs and such-like noises. The nervous show dog is easy. In most cases all he needs is a choke chain, a long lead, and a few quick sharp jerks when he sits back fearfully. That, coupled with a confident happy tone of voice and plenty of love when he comes on, soon does the trick. Being a show dog he has probably never worn a choke chain for fear of spoiling his ruff of hair round his neck, or some such beauty points. Secondly, the owner has never obedience-trained the dog for fear he will sit in the show

Owners fear that a choke chain will damage the hair of a long-coated breed, or they fear that it will blacken the coat of a white dog like a Samoyed. This is not true.

ring instead of standing. But in omitting obedience training the owner has forgotten it is just as easy to teach a dog to stand, as it is to sit, and that is part of the training curriculum. Obedience training of some sort should be given to all dogs whether they be show dogs or just household pets.

I think it is rather cruel to force a dog to be sociable to someone he doesn't like, but all dogs should be taught to allow themselves to be handled on the command: "Stand", in case the vet has to examine the dog. So the sooner he learns this exercise the better. But I fail to understand why people complain that their dog will not be friends with strangers. Who wants a dog to be friendly with strangers? As long as he is polite and well-behaved surely that is enough? If however you have a show dog the judge is always impressed by a nice happy, friendly dog; he hates risking being bitten by a nervous one. In any case I think it quite wrong to show a very nervous dog. Bad temperament should be heavily penalised so that owners are not encouraged to breed with him and pass on this fault. If an adult dog shows nerves what good is he as a sire? However many beauty points he may possess, he can never be a first-class dog.

When I get a nervous dog here that won't be handled by strangers or a judge, the first thing I do is to put a choke chain on him. This very often has a devastating effect on the owner, who immediately has visions of all her precious Afghan's hair being rubbed off, or her Samoyed's hair turning black where the choke chain meets the neck and it takes me a long time to convince owners that if the choke chain never

closes on the neck, which is my method, how can it damage hair? I teach my owners to throw their hands forward, jerk and let go with the left hand, still keeping the right hand on the lead. In fact we almost have a ditty when everyone says: "Throw the hands forward, jerk and let go" together before we start using the choke chain. Unless the hands are thrown forward you don't get the lead loose enough to allow the quick jerk. The dogs should not even see the jerk, it should be so quick. The next excuse I get from nervous or disbelieving owners is that they haven't the strength to jerk a big dog. I point out that strength is not needed. I myself have an injured spine after a car accident, yet I can jerk a large St Bernard and get the same result as I get with a tiny Papillon or Yorkie. It is a knack which is vital to learn. Sometimes I put the choke chain on my own wrist and act as the dog for the owner to practise on so that the poor dog should not suffer the incorrect jerks the owner gives until she has been really indoctrinated with the correct quick action.

Let us take the cases of nervous dogs which won't allow the judge or stranger to approach them and open their mouths. My first instruction is for the owner to learn the correct tone of voice and the command: 'Talk', for it will be on this word 'Talk' that the whole training is based. This the dog must, if necessary, learn the hard way. If, on pointing to the person he is to allow to handle him, he backs away, he is jerked back into position, given a most loving tickle on the ribs at the side of the body which is kept up throughout the initial training, and again jerked back into

Show Champion Raycroft Socialite, owned by Ralph Dunne, was Crufts Supreme Champion in 1991. It takes time to build up a rapport with a dog so that it is confident enough to let a judge examine it.

position if he backs away. He soon gets tired of being jerked back and resignedly stands. Then he gets enormous praise in a fairly high-pitched voice which is opposite to the low commanding tones of the order: 'Talk'. It is quite essential for the owner to stand away from the dog. No show dog here is allowed to be strung up on his leash; they have to stay standing on the command: "Wait", then be placed, then the owner has a loose lead and stands at least eighteen inches away from the dog. I loathe to see exhibitors forever placing their dogs. Place them, leave them, and relax. If you train a dog to do this stand every day for a few minutes he will soon learn. I believe it is quite possible to get this behaviour in a few minutes with the right confidence from the trainer. People who come here with phobias about their dogs not liking men or not liking judges need to cast that idea out of their minds and believe the dogs will do as they are told.

Tickling tummies slowly and gently works wonders. Never use a rubbing motion, this makes dogs bad tempered. A gentle tickle with the tips of the fingers is all that is necessary to induce calm in a dog. I hate strangers who go up to dogs with their hands held to the dog's nose, usually palm towards themselves. How does the dog know with this action the hand doesn't hold something horrid? The palm should always be shown to the dog and should go straight down to between the dog's front legs and tickle gently with a soothing voice to accompany the action. Very often the dog raises its back leg in a scratching movement, he gets so much pleasure from it. The person acting as the judge in the training session must walk around the dog appraising him from all angles. Then he must go up to the dog, when the owner then gives the command: "Talk" and points towards the judge with an upward swing of the finger. This usually raises the dog's head which improves the general outline. If the dog sits back, give the lead to the person doing the supposed judging and make him step back quickly giving quite sharp but small jerks on the lead with the word: "Come". The dog may play up; if so it is essential to continue this backward movement, often changing direction until the dog realises he has got to co-operate. Then the dog's head must be handled, the chest scratched and the teeth examined. Very seldom does the dog object to this after my instructions are carried out. If more owners handed the lead to their friends and helpers when the dog refuses to be handled, the trouble would be solved very quickly. I have often cured a nervous dog in less than thirty minutes by this firm compulsion method.

Bangs and noises that terrify dogs are a constant source of trouble to dog owners. Guy Fawkes' night is a night of terror for dog and owner. So may be a walk in the town or country when a backfire may make the dog slip his lead and disappear for hours or even for ever. How is the owner to blame for this state of affairs? The answer is that familiarity breeds contempt, and if the owner takes the trouble to make these noises quite familiar to the dog during the day, the dog will soon ignore them, or even enjoy them. I trained Juno, my former Great Dane, who was a shivering mass of terrors when I bought her, to love gun-fire. I had a toy pistol with caps and played with it as a game, fired it and said: "Attack" and had a rough and tumble game with her. Soon she connected the game with the bang and became used to it and enjoyed it. Then if anyone fired a gun she looked so beautiful, obviously longing to go and attack or have a game. I used also to drop heavy books unexpectedly, and then I praised her and laughed with her; dogs love laughter and smiles like children do. I always clapped my hands when she did right and she soon connected clapping with my happy voice and smiling face. If you make odd bangs and noises at intervals, your dog will soon forget his fear. A phobia, usually suffered in smaller breeds, is the dog that won't go near another dog. The owners are usually of the shy type themselves and the dogs are only mirroring the owner's lack of really wishing to be gregarious. The best way to teach this type of dog to ignore other dogs, but to walk with them and past them without leaping away, is to use two dogs, put both on choke chains and just jerk them forward with small leaps at a very fast pace. They can't do otherwise than go together if this is done. Then drop the leads, give a thunderous command: "Wait" and the dogs are usually so surprised at the tone of voice and backward hand signal over their heads that they stand quite still for a few seconds. With repeat performances of this, the dogs ignore each other and other dogs and are on the road to a cure.

I think the word 'won't' is the word I hate most in dealing with dogs with phobias. In my opinion there is no such thing as 'won't'. There may be an initial "can't" in the early stages of training, but "won't" is made up by the owner to cover a multitude of excuses, none of which I tolerate. In my opinion if the word 'won't' is allowed to excuse bad behaviour and nothing changes that attitude, the dog is not worth keeping, for the dog would be unhappy in the world of "won't" and the owner ineffective and unlikely to get much joy from the dog. It is for this reason I always take the dog away from the owner for a few minutes at the first meeting and show the owner he *will* do what he is asked if the right tone of voice is used, the right happy attitude of mind cultivated, and above all the really happy praise that the dog gets when he does as is wanted. In praising dogs I always use the words: "What a good dog". I have lined a class of dogs up and told the owners to praise them in their usual manner, then told them to prefix the praise with the word: 'What' and the effect on the dogs is undeniable. For some extraordinary reason the word: 'What' electrifies them and gives them so much more pleasure than ordinary praise. I have dozens of letters saying it really does work after I had told listeners in a broadcast to say this to their dogs.

Chapter Four

PERSISTENT BARKING

Persistent barking can often be cured and I do not think it should ever be endured. A dog barks because it is bored, hysterical or nervous; because it is spoilt and pining for affection; because it is fierce, or because it is just plain stupid. The first step must be for the owner to decide which category the dog belongs to before it is possible to diagnose the trouble and offer a solution for curing it. The last two categories are rare but there are, unfortunately, some dogs that are either really fierce, or stupid to the point of imbecility. These are the most difficult cases of all, and in my opinion, if such dogs bark persistently, nothing can usefully be done; it is kinder to put them away.

Bored, hysterical or nervous dogs are most frequently found among those that spend the major part of their lives chained up; such dogs always tend to bark to attract attention, and because their interests are so restricted that they are on edge with boredom. The slightest noise sets them off. Keeping a dog chained up like this is extremely unkind: if he is wanted as a watch-dog he can carry out that duty just as well from behind a large wire run, though even a dog penned in like this should be taken out and given a long run at least once a day. Plenty of exercise is really the answer, for a tired dog will not bark. Apart from exercise it also helps for this type of dog to mix a lot with human beings and occasionally also with other dogs; they become much more placid when they have been taken out and about.

The type of dog that causes most trouble is the spoilt one belonging to an over-sentimental owner. Some cases are caused after the period following a long spell of serious illness or quarantine when the owner is, kindly but quite mistakenly, doing everything she can to 'make it up to the dog for all it has suffered'. Dogs don't understand that kind of thing; they simply put it down to softness on the part of the owner. They lose all respect for her and consider they can play her up whenever they feel like it. Instead of lying quietly in their beds as they are told when the owner leaves the room at night, they bark and whine and make everybody's life a misery. It is your duty to stop this noise

Dogs that are chained up live on the edge of boredom and the slightest noise starts them barking.

today. Whenever the dog barks in the course of the day you should give him a really good shaking on the choke chain and make him lie down in a voice that is unrelenting and authoritative. If he is then good and quiet, you must be sure to praise him generously. At night, by showing both firmness and love, you must get the dog to lie quietly in his basket when you leave the room and, should he either get up or bark, you must rush back just once and scold him really fiercely. You must sound very angry and once you have left the room for the second time you must not come back however much the dog may bark or whine.

Over-sentimental owners often fail in this treatment. They find it difficult to get a sufficiently stern note into their voice, and they also keep asking themselves: 'Can there be something wrong with him? Should I go back to make sure?' when they ought to harden their hearts against the frustrated dog's barking. In such cases the help of a professional trainer should be sought. Some owners think trainers maltreat dogs; in fact they simply make the dog understand, where the owner seems incapable of doing this, that no nonsense will be tolerated. When I ran a residential training school for dogs and owners, the dogs were put to bed in kennels built into the rooms. The owner would put the dog to bed but was not allowed to return to the dog if he barked. I used to go once to the room to scold the dog and then to comfort him, after which it was left to its own devices. The dog found the scolding unpleasant; he also found that making a noise didn't bring the owner back. It sometimes took two days for the lesson

to sink in, but we always won in the end. Most people imagine they are being very firm with their dogs and are really surprised when I tell them that both their voices and their attitude to their dogs are rather more like blancmange than like anything else. I am never angry; I just put on an act. Dogs understand.

One of the most difficult vices to overcome is that of the dog who will not be left alone. This takes longer to cure than most faults, because it is the owner who must be cured - of lack of firmness. Daily firmness is essential. The dog must be taught to lie down and stay down. When he gets up the owner must return to him and sound cross, and put him down again. There must be no let-up on this. The dog must be made to stay down in spite of piercing shrieks or whines. It may be necessary to give him a firm jerk as he is put 'down' on the choke chain. If he barks give the command "Cease" - and mean it. Tone of voice is everything in this case. Occasionally I have found the words "Shut up" extremely effective if snapped out. There must be no pleading with the dog to stay, for that won't help. But when he does stay, even for a few minutes, the praise must be terrific.

Always remember dogs cannot bark for long lying down, they get tired. Therefore whenever a dog makes a nuisance of himself by barking make him lie down. This is quite the most important exercise in dog training. If necessary, you must sit down on a chair and put the dog, with his lead on, into the down position on the floor beside you. Then run the lead under the arch of your shoe. If the dog attempts to get up, give the command "Down" and

A dog cannot bark for long if it is lying down.

tighten the lead by pulling it upwards from where it runs under your shoe. By this method the dog's head is pulled gently to the ground, and he must sooner or later lie down unless he wishes to choke himself. Try not to have to bend down yourself; it is better that the dog shouldn't connect you with what is going on. When he does lie down, say something nice to him and show you are pleased, but not in an excited tone of voice or he will get up again. When the exercise is over then give him a real petting.

Do this exercise for a few minutes to start with, eventually sitting the dog down for half an hour. Never relent whilst doing this exercise. Remember that if the dog obeys, the choke chain will immediately release itself, so it is within the dog's power to be comfortable. I cannot repeat too often that to make a problem dog good, you must have a strong will. Let the dog win and you are further back than when you started. Leave the dog in the 'down' position for longer periods at a time each day. When he trusts that you are going to come back, the trouble of never being able to leave him alone in the house does not occur. Smacking is useless, scolding is only a little better. It is the quiet firmness that wins, never failing to put him back and down where he came from. Occasionally a 'put on' cross voice will steady a nervous dog, but never lose your temper. This exercise is just as much a test of the owner's character as the dog's. Weak people never win. Remember this trouble is probably your fault in the first place; it is up to you to put it right. Always do everything you can to make the exercise liked by the dog. Give him his favourite blanket to lie on; if possible let him have his own chair in the sitting room. It is only when all these things fail that sterner measures have to be taken. And remember problem dogs need far sterner measures than puppies or normal nice dogs.

Now let us consider the dog that shrieks in cars. Is the owner never to go for a drive with the dog? If training has proved ineffective, what is the answer? I think it is quite simple. First, the owner must study her own driving methods. Is she a bad driver, jamming on the brakes, accelerating suddenly, turning corners sharply, cursing other motorists who do not comply with her wishes? Well, that is the sort of motorist that makes dogs scream in cars. Once I was driven at night to the film studio with Juno, my Great Dane. She had driven with me all her life, and slept most of the miles we covered. This drive was a nightmare. The driver was nervous, she made me feel my end was near at least ten times in twenty-two miles. The dog picked up my nerves, braced her feet against the car door at every corner or red light, panted and showed obvious distress. Had she been a young dog she might have barked or whined in fear. The car was too small to allow me to turn round and comfort her, and the result was that we were wrecks when we arrived at our destination. This one drive with a bad driver had been enough to make my dog frightened, after which if I inadvertently braked suddenly, she lost confidence and showed distress. It took me some weeks to get her confidence back by driving steadily.

Doesn't it make one realise how easily a highly-strung dog can get in this state of nerves all the time if the driver of the car it is in is erratic? Therefore the first thing I would do if I had a dog that jumps or shrieks, is to reassess my own standard of driving. Make an effort to drive with more thought for the nerves of the dog, as well as for the safety of other road-users. In connection with this, it often occurs that the husband of the driver, or the wife, nags perpetually whilst being driven, or automatically jams down an imaginary footbrake. No one thinks that either of these two things affect a dog, but they do. The mind of the dog is acutely tuned to all brain reactions of its owners, and a sense of anger or frustration on the part of a member of the family is quickly communicated to the dog.

Having examined your driving methods and found them perfect, the next thing to do is to think how the dog can be kept quiet whilst you and your family enjoy yourselves. Fighting the dog in the car will only bring forth anger from some member of the family – unless you are all saints – and in any case, any disturbance whilst driving is dangerous in these days of congested motoring, so I am not going to suggest that kind of cure. But what possible harm can there be in keeping tranquillisers for the dog? I don't recommend these as an alternative to training, but in this instance we are discussing a situation where training has failed, probably due to the over-sentimentality of the owner. But even an over-sentimental owner cannot object to a tranquilliser or confining the dog to a folding kennel. I can instantly hear people saying: "But what happens if I only want to go on short journeys? The tranquilliser wouldn't have time to work and would probably last long after my journey is over." Well, the answer to that is, why take the dog along with you? It is quite obviously no pleasure for you or the dog, so leave him at home where he is presumably happy. Then I hear the words "Oh, he shrieks at home if he is left by himself." The only answer is to muzzle the dog, if all training fails.

Some of these problem dogs are given away as being unmanageable – and a new home and owner can work wonders. The dog gets less nervy if the new owner understands how to manage him, and he at once becomes a happy dog. There is no doubt about it, many owners and dogs are complete misfits, and the dog will never be happy or sane with them. If only the owners had to pass some sort of test before being paired up with a dog, many unfortunate dogs would have better owners and many unlucky owners would have nicer dogs.

Chapter Five

VICIOUS DOGS

All too often an owner lets a dog get away with biting, thinking that is is just puppy-play. So many owners let this habit grow until the dog is master of the situation! It is over-sentimental owners who produce biting dogs, and few of these on their own, even with instruction, can cure this vice. They need expert help, for the cure is to return violence with violence. If you are going to attempt to cure him yourself, put the dog on a long piece of string attached to its choke chain. When it attempts to bite, the person it goes for should pick up the string and suspend the dog for a few seconds off its front legs, leaving its back feet on the ground, and at the same time by using a thunderous tone of voice should make it very clear to the dog that its actions are quite unwarranted, and in no way going to be tolerated. The dog while suspended thus will feel like choking and will quickly realise who is master of the situation. Do not put the dog back on its front legs until it shows signs of discomfort (usually after about ten seconds). Now the dog will be subdued, and you should caress and praise it.

Repeat this process every time the dog persists in the habit; you will certainly have to do so two or three times if the vice is deeply ingrained. A dog despises you if it bites you, so you must force it to respect you. I know it sounds cruel, but it is not, and is much kinder than putting a dog to sleep, to which further biting might well lead.

Some dogs are over-protective towards their owners, and although they are sweet-natured to their owner, they bite anyone else who approaches. This is a trait that many dogs have, especially German Shepherds and Corgis. It is part of their shepherding instinct and if not checked young is quite incurable. The owners enjoy it at first instead of severely scolding their dogs, and by the time the dog is about eighteen months old it is difficult to stop. If only I could get inside the mind of a dog with this problem, I have no doubt he would give me a long account of over-soft attentions that it never asked for. I feel certain that if, as a puppy, it tried to do naughty things, the owner would have spoken gently to the dog like a child, never losing his temper or raising a

A dog that attacks without provocation is probably mentally unstable.

finger to the dog, believing this was the kindest way to treat a dog, and would ensure that the dog became a wonderful companion as it grew up. This type of owner probably believed that the dog would reward them with instant, happy obedience. How wrong can you be!

Dogs are not like children; they are like dogs. They need to be treated like dogs until they have graduated to being like children. A dog must be trained firmly, and shown your love unmistakably when it does right. The dog should have been shaken hard when it threatened to bite. It is never too late to learn, but the owner needs to change his attitude towards the dog. The dog must learn to respect its owner Familiarity breeds contempt. You have been too familiar with your dog before he learnt to behave. In order to cure the dog of biting, take it, muzzled if necessary, amongst crowds, and this is the first step towards curing the habit. Get people to touch the dog when it is muzzled, and give the dog a terrific scolding if it attempts to attack. If this fails get someone who trains dogs to snatch the dog from you and really shake it when it shows signs of being vicious. He must be defeated, then praised.

Some dogs show a dislike for children, which, at worst, culminates in a desire to attack them. This problem arises primarily from fear. Take the dog where children are coming out from school, playing fields, etc; daily doses of this will soon make familiarity breed contempt. Make sure first, though, that subconsciously the owner doesn't also hate children. If this is the case get someone who loves children to take the dog out and amongst them for you,

someone who trusts the dog and won't automatically tighten the lead when children approach. If there is any risk of the dog biting a child, muzzle it. I always fail to understand why people imagine muzzles are cruel; they are of the greatest help in training a dog, for when the dog is muzzled the owner's mind can be carefree. Time and time again I have met people who quake in their shoes and protest when I muzzle a dog, yet in a few minutes the dog pays no attention to the muzzle and plays happily in it; most unstable dogs would be happier with a muzzle and a less worried owner.

I can never understand people who ring me up and ask my advice on what to do with a dog that has seriously bitten a child more than once. My answer must always be that that dog is a beastly minded dog, so why take the risk of injury to your family? Obviously the owner is incapable of training it or it would never have reached this state of retaliation. For dogs are only driven to bite under such circumstances because they despise people - the result of not having been trained by them to do anything interesting or useful. But there is a worrying trend of dogs that suddenly and quite unexpectedly, turn on their owners. These are often dogs that have been faithful and contented companions for some time, and distraught owners phone me to know what to do. It is extremely difficult to help people over the phone, for it may be one of many things that makes a dog suddenly revert to this type of retaliation, but I am always suspicious that this is another case of schizophrenia.

The usual symptoms are a complete

lack of warmth in the eye, as if the dog had a headache, the lower lids often become red and the eyes have no depth to them. The inside of the ears become red as if the dog had a toxaemia and a frightful headache. He may suddenly bite viciously the person he has previously loved most, and then some minutes later be perfectly normal; the ears return on the inside to a pale colour, the eyes get their depth and look of love back again, and I am sure the dog does not remember biting at all. I myself had forty-six stitches in one arm and sixteen in another from a Bulldog which I had been training. He did all the exercises to perfection and had been a very loving and lovable chap. I had him in a field on a lead, talking to his owner; he was behind me when suddenly I didn't know what had hit me. This animal leapt on to my right arm and bit right down to my tendons, a millimetre more and I would have been a cripple for life in that arm. I managed with superhuman effort to get his mouth open and he got me on the other hand and bit that to the bone. Then he dropped off, wagged his tail and obviously expected the loving treatment he had had throughout his training. It was only then that the owner told me he had bitten her five times. The vet agreed with me that this was schizophrenia and put the dog to sleep.

I feel sure many of these unprovoked attacks which kill children or do some terrible damage to human beings are cases of schizophrenia. I once told the owner of a Labrador to put his dog to sleep when he described unprovoked aggression in the dog, and he said his wife would be heartbroken if he did that, and he was going to give it another chance. Ten days later the dog bit his small child, who was terribly injured in the face. The dog was put down. I often wonder why people phone me and don't take my advice. I have no axe to grind in saying put the dog to sleep, if I really feel the dog is not safe. My first idea always is to try and train the dog. My only other method of saving the dog's life is to have it sent to the vet and have all its teeth out. One dog who bit a child four times had this done on my advice and is now eleven years old; even if it made an attack, it could do no damage.

Nobody knows the cause of schizophrenia. Many people say it is a hormone upset, many people think it a dietetic upset, but until the veterinary profession find some definite clues to its cause, whether hereditary or formed in the lifetime, no-one with a dog that behaves as I described should keep it unless muzzled, or with no teeth, for these dogs only have to get someone in an artery for that person perhaps to lose their life before help could be obtained. I am very shocked at the deterioration in dogs' temperament these days. At shows dogs should be disqualified at the slightest sign of bad temperament, but this does not happen. I have seen a bad tempered Dobermann win a challenge certificate. I have seen a very nervous Irish Wolfhound, which would not stand up properly, be placed over a beautiful dog with a wonderful temperament. I am not a show person, so I don't know what possible excuse the judge could have had for placing the dogs like this, but I think the judge should not be a judge and encourage the breeding of nervous or bad-tempered dogs. Very often the two run

A breed such as a Corgi with a useful background of work will become neurotic if it can't hunt or chase anything.

side by side.

Boredom is another problem I have to tackle in dogs. These days they have little to interest them, beyond the daily walks which are often only to the shops and back, not the woods and fields. Anyway the woods and fields are mostly empty of exciting smells and things to chase. The result is that dogs like Corgis and Spaniels with a background of useful work become neurotic, and as they can't hunt or chase anything they bite their owners. These self-same dogs, given a fixed schedule of obedience work or even just household tricks to

perform, become different characters. Unfortunately these days owners are so busy that the time taken to train a dog can hardly be spared. They hope that the dog will fit in with their household arrangements without any special training, except house manners. They get annoyed or disappointed when this is not so. The result is that the dog becomes neurotic and sometimes vicious.

Every dog, like every child, should have some routine work given it to do every day, even if only for ten minutes a day. If the dog continues to be vicious after you have trained it, there is something lacking or abnormal in its make-up, and abnormal dogs cannot safely be kept. But this does not mean the dog should be given away to a so-called 'kind home in the country' to bite other unsuspecting people. I think the owner should face up to his or her responsibility and put it to sleep, and also face up to the fact that the owner has failed the dog, and vow to learn more about dogs before having another.

Chapter Six

DOG FIGHTS

Fighting dogs are the ones that give most worry to owners. It is this vice which owners hope a psychiatrist will be able to probe and cure. But once again I stress that, since this is the process of investigating into the past of a dog's mind which cannot be probed as the dog cannot answer questions, one can't progress. That does not mean we cannot understand a dog's present state of mind. Although past events may have had disastrous effects on the dog and have affected his mind and make-up, it will have to be the owner who is psycho-analysed to find the answer to the dog's problems. But as few owners would have the nerve or sense to go to a human doctor to find out why her dog fights, I think we can leave out this subject too.

A dog fights for several reasons, usually the right to survive, whether this be taken as the right to eat and live peaceably or simply that the dog wants to live up to a certain standard whereby he has no enemies or neighbours that irritate him. We do not know which fits each individual case. What we do know is that dogs pretend to fight in play, mauling each other in a rough and tumble which nobody minds. Puppies have mock fights all the time to strengthen their limbs and develop their jaws and to wear off their super abundance of energy. But the subject we are looking at here is serious dog fighting, which is dangerous for dogs and humans, and has been known to end in death for the smaller and weaker dog. Even if the fight is not so bad as to end in death it can cause the owner of the dog to have a heart attack from fear, it can cause people to be bitten, and is most unpleasant and terrifying to say the least of it.

Most people do not realise it takes quite a few minutes for two dogs to get really to grips. Before that they are playing for a hold, and therefore, when you go to separate a dog fight, there is no need to rush in and get bitten. It is far safer to watch at close range until you can safely get a hold of collar, or loose skin between the eyes of the dog. Once it has got a hold on the other dog it is unlikely to turn round and bite the person trying to release its hold, so you are reasonably safe when it has got a

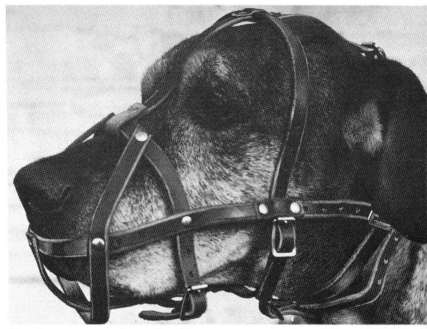

If a dog is muzzled it will realise it is at a disadvantage and will show no sign of aggression. This muzzle is perfectly comfortable for any dog.

hold in slipping a lead on, or grabbing the choke chain or scruff. It is useless beating the dog; they are mentally unaware of pain at that moment and unless you knocked the dog out you would not hurt them enough to separate them once they had a real hold. A mild dog fight, where death is not the object of the aggressor, can sometimes be stopped by beating when the dog has no collar, but the best method if two people are about is for each on the word 'now' to grab their collars and hold them off their front legs so they begin to choke; it takes terrific strength to do this with big dogs, so I grab the flesh on the forehead between the eyes and they let go at once with this. Moreover they cannot bite you.

What is in the dog's mind when it attacks every dog it meets or just has one enemy round the corner? Most of it is show of strength, very often a cowardly show of strength aimed at other people's toy dogs who can't answer the bully back. Face that same bully with a big dog likely to answer back and it will disappear into the distance, for the dog knows who will be boss even in its own race and, if it senses superiority of physique or brain, it will automatically be subservient. That is why young dogs lie on their backs, all four feet in the air when they meet an older or stronger dog; they know who is boss and are showing the other dog so by giving the 'pax' sign which is exposing the tummy to an enemy. That

This muzzle is uncomfortable to wear, and it should not be used.

is why I tell pupils that this trick is not a nice one really, and should be checked at an early age, for it is purely one of a weak animal giving in to a stronger one in mind and usually an enemy at that. Few owners would like to think their dogs look upon them as enemies, but that is the case. When a dog no longer looks upon you as a potential enemy it stops this lying on its back as protection, though many dogs in later life do it because their owners have scratched their chests which they like, and they hope for it again. But primarily it belongs to the defence mechanism of the dog tribe.

The mind of a dog that fights always has at the back of it the wish to be the boss of the tribe, and he fights other male dogs who are sexually mature to make sure there is no risk of his being questioned as 'lord of all he surveys'. Muzzle that dog and let him loose with the dog he has previously fought, and nine times out of ten, he will realise he is at a disadvantage and show no signs of aggression. That is why I muzzle fighters and free them with trained dogs or non-fighters. They then learn to enjoy themselves in a community and the wish to fight goes. Often, having muzzled, introduced and trained them for a short time together, I have formerly bad fighters lying side by side without muzzles after a few minutes. It is much easier to teach a dog to ignore others in a training class, as we divide the class into two sections, one at each end of the room; and on the command: 'Forward' they walk forward and pass through the line of dogs opposite them, so that the dogs pass beside one another. We call this exercise 'counter-marching'. As the dogs approach each other if one even looks at the other, a firm command: 'Leave' is given, and a sharp jerk on the offender's choke chain. If this exercise is repeated again and again, and the dog always receives a jerk just before he sniffs the other dog, he is left with the impression that it is rather unpleasant to talk to another dog in such circumstances. I have cured fighters by this method in a very short time.

But the real difficulty lies in knowing when your dog is going to fight; it is useless to take such steps once the dogs have come to grips with each other. How many people are sufficiently knowing with their dogs to sense the stiffening of the body which is preliminary to a fight? Too many owners usually wait until the fight has started before doing anything about it. That is why it is a good thing for an experienced trainer to have the first chance, especially in a class, to check this fighting tendency. But wherever they are, if owners really know their dogs they will sense the stiffening of the dog as he approaches another, the dog's way of sending out a warning to the other one that he is ready to hold his own against all comers. A dog that has no intention of fighting is relaxed. One that is not sure, but wishes to be friendly, keeps up a very fast but confined wagging of its tail as it approaches another dog; this will stop, and the dog will stiffen, if the enemy has evil ideas, and is not reciprocating

the offer of friendship.

Most dogs approach a bitch in this way, hoping for friendship, and although it is unusual for a dog and bitch to fight, the bitch may attack first and then the dog will answer back, but usually not for very long. A growl, of course, must never be ignored. A fight inevitably follows unless checked, but an owner must be able to read far less obvious indications than the growl and the snarl if he is to stop fights at the right moment - that is, before they have begun. This business of making your dog ignore others needs constant vigilance; a second's carelessness, and you are in a fight. I believe that if a dog does get involved in a fight he should be severely punished unless he was obviously attacked first. Therefore, as I hate to advocate punishing dogs, it is the owner's duty to see that no fight develops. It is a fatal move to tighten your lead as another dog approaches, and even worse to lift your dog up. Walk on quite naturally until reasonably near the other dog, then give a sharp jerk on your dog's collar to arrest his attention, and in a firm, low voice, command: 'Leave'. It is the most difficult thing possible to impress on owners of fighting dogs that to cure them they must have long loose leads, that holding a dog on a short lead tends to make it want to fight more. A four-foot lead is essential, and a completely indestructible clip. The scissor hook and ordinary hook are dangerous, as both can open up with a sharp jerk. For if a fighting dog did get free when jerked hard it would be twenty times worse than before, because the jerk would have sent it forward when the clip broke and would probably catapult it into the other dog. The jerks to cure fighting dogs must be hard and effective.

Quite a number of people want to know whether they can really cure a confirmed fighter so that it may safely be allowed to run freely with other dogs. I should say no. A dog can be so far cured as to be safe at all times when under the control of its owner. We have often trained fighters to be safely left in a hall with thirty or more other dogs lying all together, all the owners out of sight, but all the dogs in the room had had training, therefore the fighter was not getting challenges or rude remarks thrown at it by other dogs. However, I would not like to say that the former fighter, if attacked, would not fight to the finish. I think he would, and only a terrific amount of disciplinary training would make it safe at all times. I have cured (to the point of their becoming very nice dogs to take out without a lead) dogs that were previously bad fighters; one had even killed another dog, but it had a sensible owner. It must depend to a great extent on the owner's temperament. If the owner is always nervous, the dog will always be on his guard against aggression; if the owner is confident that her dog is cured of its vice, the dog will gain assurance from that attitude, and be far less likely to want to fight.

I think fighting, with biting of owners, postmen and visitors, are all attributable together to the one complaint: nerves and insecurity. The dog has probably not been taken out and about enough in its youth. To make a dog reliable, it should be taken into towns and crowds, shops and parks, and wherever you live, it must be allowed to meet other dogs. Let people caress it and talk to it. Be firm if it slinks away and won't talk to people; show it that human beings are its friends. If possible, find a friendly neighbour's dog and let it have romps with it, making sure that on command it leaves off playing and comes back to you. Such a dog will never be a fighter: why should it be? Big dogs are often put on a very short lead and held in a vice-like grip in the street. Times without number I have shown owners that a fighter on a loose lead seldom attacks, but they are so scared that they daren't let up on the stranglehold. Naturally, if you get a big dog involved in a fight, it takes plenty of courage and strength to end the battle. I once separated two dogs, and then one got hold of my leg, thinking it was the other dog, and I couldn't let go of the second or the fight would have started all over again. Luckily someone took one dog from me while I prised the other off my leg, but I still bear the scar.

I think fighting is, to a certain extent, an inherited temperamental fault, and I strongly advise buyers of dogs to enquire about the parents' temperaments before buying a puppy. Fighters are always of a bullying nature, and therefore need a strict code of discipline from an early age. Any sign of rolling on their backs, and biting the owner or its lead when the lead has to go on, is often the prelude to serious biting or fighting later in life. I am always dead against allowing a dog to use its teeth on me even in play, and any attempt to answer back with its teeth when I give a command is instantly checked. I often feel that dogs bite and fight to let off steam. Many live such restricted lives that they become psychological cases

Dog owners can be rash in the breed they choose – it is important to find out what job of work a dog was bred for as this will affect its temperament.

weighed down by repressions. In such circumstances, human beings lose their tempers or burst into tears, but dogs are allowed no such outlet. I feel that a dog that leads a fully occupied life as a complete member of the owner's family never gets these vices, having plenty of legitimate interests to keep it stable.

I know of one household that owns two dogs, one a Staffordshire Bull Terrier, and one a charming old Fox Terrier. The two dogs belong respectively to the husband and wife, but never the twain shall meet, for the Staffordshire has only one idea in its head and that is to annihilate the old age pensioner and reign supreme alone in that household. He only developed this hatred for the Fox Terrier when he grew up. As a puppy he was all right. What should the owners do to make life liveable with two dogs, neither of which they wish to part with? I feel that as this situation has been allowed to develop over quite a long period of time, no very practical training has been carried out. The easiest way out has been taken by separating the dogs and dividing the household in two. I would give the Bull Terrier a course of obedience training, and take it out and about to meet other dogs as often as possible. I would fix up a very strong chain and collar near its bed or basket and make it lie down and stay down in that whenever the two members of the family wish to be in that room with the Fox Terrier. If the dog growled or showed signs of jealous temper I would jerk it hard on the choke chain giving simultaneously the command: 'Leave'. Then I would pet it. I would take the dogs out together on leads with the Bull Terrier wearing temporarily a Greyhound type of muzzle. No possible damage could then occur to the old dog, and I believe that by enjoying their walks together they would become friendly. I would never pet one in front of the other without speaking lovingly to them both.

One often hears of Spaniels, especially mother and daughter, who so hate each other that one has to be put to sleep to gain peace. This is terribly sad, and, on the part of the owner, an admission of failure to teach them obedience. You cannot make them love each other, any more than I can teach dogs to love their owners, but you can teach them to ignore each other by successful obedience training. The same sort of thing arises when people get a new kitten or puppy. How can they train the other animal to tolerate and accept it? This is not a very difficult problem if the newcomer is small enough to confine in an indoor kennel or cage at night, with the old dog chained to his bed near the newcomer, for I have found that when animals share the night in close proximity to each other they seldom are at war afterwards. Again, of course, the old well-known command: 'Leave' comes into the training, and by this time the dog should know that word means 'ignore everything and don't chase anything'.

It is, in all these cases, the attitude of the owner that matters. Occasionally I discover the owner is neurotic, and rather enjoys her dog disliking her husband's dog, though she wouldn't admit it. More troubles with dogs are caused because they are mirroring inhibitions with idiosyncrasies of their owners than we know about. That is why it is very difficult for me to diagnose what is wrong with a dog or owner when I only have a letter to read. Although in the end one becomes like a psychologist and quickly sees under the veneer put on for one's benefit. Over-possessiveness on the part of the owner causes many dogs to do naughty things. The owner who never lets her dog romp with another for fear of picking up something, or the dog that is never allowed a good race over the fields because it gets its newly-shampooed self dirty, is asking for trouble. Even toy dogs like Yorkshire Terriers or Pekinese love a rat hunt. A dog becomes a dull creature with nothing but town walks and chauffeur-driven rides in the park. In my school, when the weather permits, we take all the so-called problem dogs into a field, and in spite of protests from owners who feel certain their dogs will fight or get eaten alive, or won't come when called, we let the whole lot go free at the same time. So far we have never had anything terrible happen. Sometimes a fight is imminent, but my voice can usually avert it, and soon the owners become confident and willing to trust their dogs, and that is the first step towards a happy dog and owner relationship. Good behaviour is undoubtedly infectious, and it is quite amazing to see how good these 'difficult dogs' are in school. If only one could instil the methods of control sufficiently into the owners they would be no trouble at home either. I think lack of time is the main enemy. Practice makes perfect. Working dogs only once a week is useless.

I think dog owners can be rash in the breed of dog they choose. I wish they would find out more about what the dogs were originally bred for, before they buy one. All the bull-breeds were bred for fighting in one way or another, also the Irish Terriers and Kerry Blues. Why do weak little owners want this type of dog? Is it that they lack courage in their make-up and buy a courageous dog to compensate? If you are a flat-dweller choose a dog that needs little exercise or work like the King Charles Spaniel, whose ancestors are so often pictured in old oil paintings and whose lives in various courts of royalty were well known. I have met a family who expected a Beagle to lead this sort of life and who complained when it became unmanageable. One Beagle in a family of children must be a misfit. They are hunting dogs, not playthings, and they have very stubborn natures. The choice of dog must of course rest with the buyer, but I do feel breeders could refuse to sell an old lady a Bloodhound, or a small child a big boisterous breed. I suppose those who breed dogs do so for profit, and few can afford to refuse a sale. I only wish they had the dogs to deal with when they become problem dogs, and it would then deter them from selling unsuitable dogs.

If a dog continues to fight at the slightest pretext after an owner has followed all my recommendations, I should say he was incurable, and the owner must decide whether to keep him, and always be on guard against a fight, and the risk of his causing harm which may end up in the law courts, or whether to have him put to sleep to end his unhappy existence. I hate to advocate putting a dog down at any time, and only the owner can decide on a matter of this kind. Most fighters are what they are through bad handling by inexperienced owners. Once the habit is firmly established it takes an experienced handler to cure it, but a fighting dog is an unsafe dog at all times, even a partially 'cured' one.

Any sort of work will make a dog more interested in its owner, and therefore less inclined to roam.

Chapter Seven

ROAMING DOGS

How irritating it must be never to know where your dog is! Or to own a dog that perpetually wishes to go off on his own pursuits. How does this happen? It comes about for many reasons. The first is that many people imagine it is cruel to confine a dog to the house with you, and that dogs can't be happy without their freedom. It comes about because people own dogs and haven't the time to exercise them, or the time to look after them, and they take the easiest way out by opening the front door and letting their dogs go out on their own, knowing they will return when tired or hungry. These people lack imagination, they do not visualise what might happen in those hours the dog is running free on his own pursuits. They never think that their dog may cause a human being to die in a car accident, nor do they visualise the dog getting injured and lying uncared for on the road. They have never thought that their male dog may mate with some tiny uncared for bitch on heat and cause her to suffer or die having puppies too big for her. They do not think of the risk of their dog picking up infection. All they like is to have a dog to bark at intruders at night and to play occasionally with the children. They have no idea what they miss. They do not know what heights of intelligence can be reached by a dog. They should never own a dog. A cat would suit them better, for cats prefer being allowed to roam when the spirit moves them, and most cat lovers agree that it is not kind to confine a cat too closely; although I think cats would also miss the deep affection this type of owner never bestows on an animal.

How can one cure a roaming dog? First of all by training. Any sort of work makes a dog more interested in his owner. Having the dog with you when you shop, when you go in the car, when you are in the home, all tend to make the dog rely on you for all his needs. But there are some male dogs tortured by the sex urge, and if there is a bitch on heat within five miles I have heard owners complain their dog knows and is a menace. My answer to that is, castrate him. The roaming instinct is also the reason why the dogs do not come to their owners' call when out for exercise. This is a major problem and a large percentage of my correspondence is about it. The owners often say the dog is good and obedient in the house or garden, but get him outside where smells abound, or other dogs roam, and the dog becomes completely deaf to orders. What can they do?

They must put their dog on a long lead and a choke chain and take him where there are plenty of distractions, leave him at the sit and walk away from the dog to the fullest extent of the lead. Give the command: "Come" prefacing all commands with the dog's name; if the dog looks about elsewhere or doesn't literally leap to his feet to obey, give him a very sharp jerk towards you, and when he comes love him for all you are worth. The whole training depends on the way you jerk. The choke chain running end must be under the dog's chin, for in this way the jerk comes on the top of the neck – which is very muscular – and couldn't possibly cause any injury or pain to the dog; but it *does* give the dog a shock, and I have known Poodles and similar nervous dogs to give a squeal. This is not pain but shock, and you must carry on: the dog will soon learn that if he comes quickly he gets much love and praise, if he doesn't come quickly he gets an almighty jerk and has to come anyway. I reckon it only takes a few minutes to teach a dog to come when called.

Occasionally a very tough, stubborn dog will not learn this way, and then once more you have to have co-operation from a friend who should if possible have a dog with her. She should have a spare long leather lead in her hand, and when your dog comes up to her dog and won't return to you when you call, she should give it a crack with the leather lead over its backside and say: "Go Back" in a horrid tone of voice. The owner should meanwhile be calling in her most endearing tone of voice, and there is soon no doubt at all in the dog's mind which is the best place. I find this is easily taught in class in an enclosed field, because when there are twenty or more pupils all willing to help the owner whose dog won't come when called, by slapping him with a leather lead if he comes their way, the dog finds it most unpleasant to be away from his owner and safety. I hate having to do this to disobedient dogs, but these measures have to be meted out to dogs who don't love their owners. For make no mistake, if your dog doesn't come when called you take only second place in his mind to smells or other dogs. Otherwise the old trick of calling him and running away from him would be effective. He would think you were going to leave him and he would love you so much he would not want you out of his sight, and would run after you. You could then give the command: "Sit" and catch him. No, if your dog does not come it means he doesn't respect you, and without respect you have no true love from your dog.

Force in any form is repulsive to many dog owners, and I heartily agree with them. I often have to use these more forceful measures to teach the dogs obedience to their unloved owners, and I also feel revolted at having to do it, but it is my duty to help to train these dogs, and if the dogs couldn't care less whether their owners jumped into the sea or not, what can one do? I always find these dogs will come instantly to my call, which is very annoying for the owners, but then I am sending out by telepathy not only the 'or else' message, but my tremendous faith in them and my deep love for them when they behave well. Too many owners try to catch their dogs when they approach. I tell them to raise their hands up to their own chests and not use them menacingly to grab their dogs. Without the hands waving about the dogs will come right up close to the owners' knees and should sit on command, when the owners can drop down and kiss and love them for coming. I can't tell owners often enough that dogs love being kissed, they adore contact with the human face. Should titbits ever be given to a dog on returning to its owner? With a puppy I think so, and occasionally with an adult dog, but not as a rule, or the dog may get fed up and go off again when you have nothing to give one day. The right firm tone of voice when the command: "Come" is given, the immense show of love when the dog comes, and the more severe measures recommended if the dog is a stubborn one – those are the only methods I use to teach countless dogs to return instantly to their owners.

Dogs that chase moving things are a menace and must be cured at all costs. Car-chasing is one of their worst crimes. When I was in Ireland recently I noticed all the dogs in country districts chased cars. Nobody seemed to do anything about it, and the dogs were incredibly clever at avoiding getting run over. I am glad to say the dogs in this country that chase cars are the exception rather than the rule. But when they do get this dangerous habit they undoubtedly cause many accidents. How can it be stopped? The quickest and most efficient way I know is to enlist the aid of a friend with a car. Ask him to drive you slowly past the dog that chases cars, and as the dog comes in to the attack throw out as hard as you possibly can any fat, hard-covered book, and make certain that the book hits the dog. The shock it gives the dog so frightens it that I have never had to repeat the treatment more than twice, even though the dog may have chased cars for years. My favourite book is an old A.A. Handbook, it is just the right size. Try not to lean out of the car to throw it as then the dog may connect you with the throwing of the book, when you want him to connect the car with the shock he gets.

If the dog has only just developed the car or motor-bike chasing vice, a long cord on a choke chain and a terrific jerk as he goes to chase the vehicle works a cure, but an old hand at the game knows when he is on the cord and won't do it. Shepherds always say a sheep-chaser is quickly taught to leave sheep alone by being penned with a fierce ram, and chicken-chasers with a turkey cock, but I wouldn't like to bet on that. The old idea of giving the dog a kick was always stupid and cruel, I thought. For one thing the dog quickly learnt to avoid the kick as the Irish dogs learnt to avoid being hit by a car. But a book thrown with skill can reach the dog every time, and frighten him without the risk of injuring it. I recently cured a Corgi that chased motorcycles by getting the motorcyclist to carry a jug of water in one hand and throw it over the dog as she came in to chase the motor-cycle. It took three dousings to cure her, but now she shrinks back into the ditch at the approach of a motorcycle, and this may well have saved her life. All chasing of vehicles and livestock can be stopped by proper training in the recall exercise. A dog should never be so far away from his owner that he cannot be recalled. No dog should be off the lead on the highway these days, there is too much traffic. If the dog shows the least excitement at the approach of a vehicle he should be given a sharp jerk and the command: "Leave".

No dog should ever be free where there is livestock unless the owner is absolutely certain his dog will stay to heel. Far too many owners look upon farmers' fields as their natural right of way and allow their dogs to wander out of hearing before they attempt to call them in to heel. If the dog is constantly taken amongst traffic and livestock on the lead, the novelty soon wears off and the chasing does not occur. If only owners would think ahead and be alive to the risk that their dog may chase livestock, I feel sure it would never happen. The fact remains that many people encourage their dogs to chase things, and the poor dog has to learn what he can chase and what he cannot. Some dogs drive their owners mad by chasing birds on the lawn, some by running up and down the garden fence when people or dogs or vehicles go by. What is the cure? Keep the dog in away

from temptation. I find a vast number of people whose dogs have many vices prefer to grumble rather than remove the source of vice. They obviously haven't the skill to train their dogs, so they must do the next best thing and keep the dog out of the way of temptation. Take for example the bitch that destroys everything in the house. Surely the best way to stop it is to confine her when you are not about in an indoor kennel lined with zinc. She can then do no damage. If she never has a chance to destroy things she forgets the vice, and it is a good bet that she will have grown tired of doing it when she is again given the run of the house.

I honestly believe some dogs that chase things and tear things up have a mental disease. If firm training does not stop them, and giving them plenty of interest in life has no effect, then I think there is no cure. I knew one Fox Terrier who used to chase his own tail like mad every morning. On his death he was found to have a tumour on the brain. There are 'mental' human beings and 'mental' dogs. Training must not be condemned as useless until the possibility of a mental disease in the dog has been eliminated, for however good you are at training dogs, a dog with a diseased brain will never respond.

Chapter Eight

JEALOUSY

In the case of jealousy the mind of a dog works in almost an identical way to that of a human being. The dog wants the full attention and love of his owner, whether jealousy only occurs when another dog enters the home or when the beloved owner talks to another dog outside, or whether it be aimed towards another person in the home, the same driving force is at the root of the evil – the intention of the dog to reign alone and supreme in that household. The guarding instinct, so prevalent in some breeds, has its roots in the same sort of thing – a desire to let no-one enter the precincts of his master or mistress. Jealousy nearly always takes the form of a show of viciousness towards the dog or person the animal is jealous of. Quite often it is a mild form of jealousy and only involves the dog's bone, toy or piece of rug that he is fond of. He jealously guards them, and woe betide anyone trying to take the object away. This jealousy is particularly pronounced when puppies are reared and kept in the household. As the puppy reaches the age of about three months the mother will begin to feel jealous as her

maternal instinct fades and the time draws near for another 'on heat' period. In spite of trying to treat both dogs equally and always talking to both at the same time and exercising both together, the jealousy continues to grow.

Correction works at first and then bit by bit grows less effective. In the dog's mind a usurper has entered and, as in the wild state the young are turned out of the nest and abandoned, the dam is trying to do the same thing in the home. As she fails to get rid of the now grown up pup, her temper gets worse and worse in the effort to dislodge the now adult and unwanted member of the family. She becomes more and more thwarted as her owner attempts to make the newcomer as welcome as the old-established member, and often she turns on her owner when that person is trying to make peace, as if she were trying to impress an ignorant person that it was time the youngster went out to fend for itself. If you are a really good handler your training methods will be good enough to make both dogs obey the command "leave" when they are in your presence. The danger lies in

Jealousy can develop between two dogs that live together, who are competing for their owner's attention.

the times you leave the dogs together on their own, for the slightest boldness on the part of the youngster in approaching the older one's basket or toy etc infuriates the older dog, and she sets on the youngster tooth and nail. Sometimes the mother is a killer, and unless kept apart from her offspring, would no doubt have a go at killing it. Such is the age-old instinct to get rid of the young before it is time to breed again. Luckily this instinct is not very

common. Generations of domesticity have dimmed it considerably, but I have met it, mostly in smaller dogs, and I am sorry to say that I have not been able to give much hope to the owner of curing it.

Most dogs show a streak of jealousy at some time or other. When my own two dogs come to my bedroom, if I talked to the Dane, the little English Toy Terrier would jump on the bed and have a go at nipping the Dane's nose, in spite of the fact she was smiling all the time, so she would receive the pats and kisses the big one was getting, and she would also have a go, but there was a streak of jealousy in her nature which did not appear in the Dane's. But then I think little dogs possess this factor in a more marked degree than big dogs, who are more placid. Jealousy occurs when two terriers are hunting. If one catches a rat the other will often try to take it away, not because he wants it – most good ratters instantly leave their dead quarry to find other live ones – but simply because the dog is jealous, and wants to be equal with the killer. Biting of husbands or wives is a very common form of jealousy. It can be very distressing for all concerned, and as it is such an important issue I have dealt with it in a separate chapter – 'Men and Women Haters'. Dogs are seldom jealous of small children. The mind of a dog looks upon small children as it would upon its own whelps. That is why even fierce dogs are seldom known to hurt children. However, fear inevitably provokes a dog to attack, and therefore a nervous dog is always a potentially dangerous dog. That is why I curse the breeders who sell these creatures and who breed litters from problem dogs, hoping their traits won't come out in their offspring. This hope is not often fulfilled. Nervous parents teach their puppies fear by telepathy from an early age, and if the bitch feels fear, the puppies automatically follow suit. Only with training from an early age will the fear be eradicated.

Jealousy in kennelled dogs is particularly rife in stud dogs. Each stud dog wants to reign supreme over the kennel wives, and so if there are a number of stud dogs it is wise to keep them separate. Although dogs are polygamous by nature, they often choose a favourite wife. I clearly remember my German Shepherd choosing a wife and going off with her to our orchard and digging a fifteen foot underground passage and bedroom at the end for her to have her litter in; his other wives were just for business purposes, this bitch was the one true mate. She was allowed by us to have her nine puppies down there, and to see Argus standing on top of the entrance on the day she whelped was a thrilling sight. We felt the true nature of the dogs had been allowed to develop by choosing their own home, and bringing up the babies in a homely atmosphere. It was the most wonderful litter we had ever bred. But I have never seen or met with instinct like that before or since. When we opened up the nest it was beautifully made round a corner of the passage, with straw and hay the bitch had picked up in her mouth, plus masses of her own hair that she had plucked from her chest. The nest was scrupulously clean and dry; in fact she was a model many human mothers could have copied.

I don't think there is any cure for jealousy in stud dogs. I think, if some of them had the chance, they would fight to the finish, and that is too near nature for the dog trainer to be able to do an efficient job, although I do recommend muzzling and exercising them together if the breed is not too big. Naturally if dogs are properly obedience trained from the start, these things seldom occur. But the average breeder has no time or wish to carry out obedience training for fear it may spoil the

The gift of getting a dog to respond – even if the owner is a little jealous at first.

character of the show dogs. Most of us trainers know that, far from doing this, it enhances a dog's chance of winning by his perfect ring manners. I still hope the day will come when no working breed gets its championship title without also having obtained some simple obedience title. A trained dog's mind is educated; the look on his face is quite different from the scatty brutes one often sees in the ring. He has an aura of

warm, friendly confidence sadly lacking in many show dogs. The mind of a dog can absorb so much that it is child's play for him to carry out obedience exercises when wanted, and yet still remember to stand and be examined, and to run as required for the beauty ring. It only means that a few different commands are learnt, and that is no difficulty for an intelligent dog. If the dog is not intelligent, he shouldn't win prizes, for who wants a stupid dog with no mind of his own?

Now that we are on the subject of jealousy, I think that some of my pupils are a bit jealous themselves when I work their dogs. They should realise that only by years of experience have I learnt anything about training dogs; they cannot expect to work a dog without learning the art the hard way, that is hard work, patience and the willingness to learn something new every day from someone. None of us know it all, and the pupil who rushes in here with a know-all attitude will not learn as quickly as those who watch and listen, eager to assimilate knowledge. Every dog is different, and although they all undergo identical training, it is only by reading their minds and watching their reactions that progress is made. Most human pupils are wonderful the way they try patiently to follow suit in the training methods, and I think some of the dogs are beastly to be uncoperative to such loving owners, but a dog's nature is governed by a multitude of instincts and reactions, and none of us really knows it all.

Chapter Nine

MAN HATERS AND WOMAN HATERS

Why should dogs be allowed to dislike or be more frightened of men than of women or vice versa? This is the most peculiar form of instability in dogs. They seem to hate sex more than form and can be sweet and happy with a woman and nervous or vicious with the opposite sex. What form of neurosis causes this we don't know. What can an owner do to make a dog with this nature bearable? First, examine the owner's mind. Has she or he ever had a grudge against the opposite sex? Did an overpowering school mistress make the young boy or young girl's life a misery? Does she boast that she is a women's woman or does she only get on with men? "I never get on with women, my dear," is almost certainly said by the type of owner that makes a dog hate women.

German Shepherds are peculiar in this way and will hate men or women instinctively if thought transference comes from an owner with a similar dislike. So many women own German Shepherds to show their superiority over their fellow men or women. They like big guard dogs, and the big guard dog thrives under this state of affairs and develops easily a dislike of the sex the owner wishes to dominate. Corgis do the same. I have particularly noted it in these two breeds, partly because they are highly intelligent breeds and telepathy is very marked, and partly because the shepherding instinct is uppermost and they have a natural suspicion of strangers. Correct them firmly when young and one gets no further trouble. Revel in their suspicious natures and you will have dogs that hate men or women, usually women.

Now how do we live with such dogs? The world being what it is, we cannot only mix with one sex. Even husbands or wives are a necessity, and it is often against one or the other that the particular hate is centred. I think the solution is either to send the dog to be boarded or trained by a person of the sex he hates, or else get friends of the hated sex to feed the dog or take him for walks. If the dog shows any signs of being vicious, muzzle him and send him out for a long walk with the person he dislikes. Greet joyously that person when he or she returns, and praise the dog. Make the person pat the dog and praise him before saying goodbye and, if possible, give the dog his food. I know there are not many good friends who will do this for you, but I think, if an advertisment was put in the local press, some dog lover would respond. It might even help to employ a 'dog-sitter' of the hated sex, so that when you go out the only comfort the dog can get is from the sex he dislikes. Only by being made to tolerate people will he respond. Obviously if the owner has been jilted and hates all men, her dog will naturally pick up this feeling when the owner is talking to a man.

Some of the saddest letters I get come from wives with dogs that dislike their husbands; dogs that even go so far as to bite the husband, apparently without any specific reason. The cause I think is jealousy. What would I do with them? I would train the dog and the husband to respect each other's likes and dislikes. I would train the dog to go instantly to his basket and stay there when the husband is about. I would never allow the dog to lie in front of the fire and bite the husband when he moves his feet, which is a very common complaint. I would ask the husband to feed the dog, and if possible never feed the dog myself; for most animals can be won over through their tummies. I would also ask the husband to ignore the dog's lack of affection and not to force himself on the dog, however much it offends his dignity not to be liked. Very often when you ignore a dog it makes the first advances.

When a dog becomes jealous, it is usually because he senses that he is not the be-all-and-end-all of a beloved owner when the master of the house comes home, and therefore if the husband gets near his wife, he may get bitten. The answer to this one is for the husband to master the dog in no mean way, by leaving a string on his choke chain and, when he attempts to be nasty, giving him an almighty jerk and a scolding, then petting him and loving him. Then the dog will recognise that the master is the boss, and all dogs are happy to submit to a real master. Few men dare to do this with their wives' dogs for fear of upsetting their wife, or in some cases, literally being attacked by their wives in defence of the dog, for some wives would rather have their husbands bitten than allow the husbands to correct the dog. How silly can some women be? Surely the life of the family depends on the happiness of all concerned, and the dog is as much a part of the family as a child. I encourage husbands to watch their wives training their dogs, and sometimes to take over the training. It forms a happy camaraderie in the attempt to make the dog a 'joy to all and a nuisance to no one.'

In the curing of this husband-biting complex, the wife must try and feel really annoyed if the dog attacks for, make no mistake, a dog picks up the thoughts of the wife without a word being spoken, and if he thinks the wife doesn't really disapprove of having her husband bitten, then the dog will continue to do so. But if she feels angry about it, and so does the husband, the combined waves of disapproval floating about for the dog's mind to pick up will be strong enough for the most insensitive dog. Correction by the mistress of the dog in these cases seems to fail, the reason being that the dog

Breeds such as the German Shepherd have a strong guarding instinct.

doesn't respect the person he is jealous of. Otherwise he would live in peaceful co-existence. The person of whom the dog is jealous must do the correcting, and often this is an old grandmother or grandfather whose physical strength does not permit them to handle the dog in the right way. A human being must always come first in these matters or the dog will realise it is supreme and become worse and worse as his ego gets stronger support. Some breeds such as German Shepherds have a strong guarding instinct and may become over-protective towards one person.

In many cases all these faults in dogs can be traced to some minor mental disturbance of the owner, though the owner may be unaware of it. I often ignore the dog, and ask the owner searching questions to probe why the dog is unbalanced. When I find out what is wrong with the owner the dog is automatically cured. Dogs mirror their owners' inner thoughts more than their looks, as some people say. A dog mirrors your soul, for you can't deceive animals even though you may think you can. In some cases when dogs have been cruelly treated by men or women the resulting hate is purely and simply a natural fear. Then the only thing to do is train the dog firmly enough to make fear a thing of the past. Sympathy only makes things worse. Take the dog to a club with the trainer of the hated sex. If the trainer is a real dog lover, get him or her to caress and handle the dog as much as is possible in a training class. Once the dog has got confidence in a member of the hated sex you are halfway to curing him. The rest must come by constant mixing with people in crowded places where the dog hasn't time to distinguish men from women. Undoubtedly this sex hatred is not a breeding fault as so many mentally unstable faults are, so it should be easily curable with expert help. Never keep the dog away from the sex he hates, make him go amongst people all the time.

APPENDIX

A range of other books, tapes and accessories are available to help you derive the full benefit from the Barbara Woodhouse approach to dog training.

Other titles in this series are:

Barbara Woodhouse On How Your Dog Thinks

Barbara looks at the world from the dog's viewpoint, and comes up with some new and surprising theories on dog behaviour. She shows owners how to understand their dogs and to communicate with them, not just by words and commands, but by tone of voice, and body language. In this book Barbara Woodhouse uses her rare gifts to break down the barriers, and helps all owners to achieve perfect companionship with their dogs.

Barbara Woodhouse On Training Your Dog

Barbara guides the owner through the first steps of basic obedience, essential for the family pet, and graduates, stage by stage, to more advanced and specialised training. This book is essential for every owner who wants their dog to be "a pleasure to all, and a nuisance to none."

Barbara Woodhouse On Keeping Your Dog Healthy

In a lifetime spent boarding, breeding and training dogs, she has come across all the most common conditions and complaints affecting dogs, and she gives practical, no-nonsense advice on all aspects of dog care, from diet, exercise and grooming to breeding, diagnosing health problems and nursing a dog through a serious illness. When you buy a dog, you are responsible for all its physical and mental needs, and this book tells you all you need to know to be a firm, fair and loving owner.

Barbara Woodhouse On How To Train Your Puppy

IBarbara gives invaluable advice on house training, diet, exercise, and early training, and perhaps most important of all, she helps new owners get off to the right start, so that they can achieve a happy working relationship with their dog.

All these titles should be available through your local pet or book shop, price £3.99 each. In cases of difficulty they can be ordered direct from the publisher.
(Please add 75p per title towards P&P).
See address at the end of this section.

The Complete Woodhouse Guide To Dog Training

This is the definitive volume on dog training from Britain's best-loved expert. Everything you need to know about the care and control of your dog; how to understand his behaviour and how to get the best from him.
This book contains the very best of Barbara Woodhouse's writing on a subject she understands like no other.
Available from good bookshops everywhere, price £14.95

In case of difficulty The Complete Woodhouse Guide To Dog Training can be ordered direct from the publisher.
(Please add £1.50 towards P&P).
See address at the end of this section.

And if you've read the book, it is time to see the movie!

THE *WOODHOUSE* VIDEO
Barbara Woodhouse:
Quick Dog Training

A complete programme of obedience exercises for you and your dog. This 90 minute video takes you step-by-step through all the essential commands: Sit, Stay, Wait, Down, Leave and Recall.
PLUS house training, giving medicine, obedience in the car and on the street, walking to heel and much, much more from the most celebrated dog trainer in the world.

Price: £14.99
(plus £1.50 P&P)

Available ONLY from the publisher.
See address at the end of this section

BARBARA WOODHOUSE
CHOKE CHAINS AND LEADS
Are also available through the publisher

CHOKE CHAINS

Sizes at two–inch intervals
Twelve inches to eighteen inches   £3.00
Twenty inches to Twenty-eight inches   £3.50

To obtain the correct choke chain, measure over the top of the dog's
head, down over the ears and under the chin, then add two inches
and round up or down to the nearest size.
Please add 95p P&P to each order

LEADS

Approx four foot long in best quality bridle leather
Large or small trigger hooks   £5.95
Please add 95p P&P to each order

BARBARA WOODHOUSE AUDIO CASSETTE

BASED ON THE SERIES
TRAINING DOGS THE WOODHOUSE WAY
Price: £5.95
(including postage and packing)

HOW TO ORDER

All the items described here can be ordered
direct from the publisher

RINGPRESS BOOKS LTD.,
SPIRELLA HOUSE, BRIDGE ROAD,
LETCHWORTH, HERTS SG6 4ET

Please remember to add postage and packing charge where
necessary and allow 21 days for delivery.

ACCESS and VISA card holder may order by telephone on
0462 674177

Office open 9am to 5pm Monday to Friday